Acknowledgements

There have been many people who have helped and advised me in the creation of *Fundraising: The Essentials for Success*.

I want to make particular mention of Sue, my wife, whose constant proof reading and suggestions have been a major influence in keeping this concise; Iain More from whom I learnt most of what I know about fundraising, and Emma Quinn who designed this handbook and has patiently and cheerfully reset the typography times beyond number.

To all of you – very many thanks.

WHAT PEOPLE SAY

In over 40 years of fundraising in politics in the US, as Director of Development at the University of Edinburgh and INSEAD, and as the founder of and consultant for what is now the More Partnership, I have never seen a cogent, easy to read explanation of the elements of the profession I have practiced, until *The Essentials for Success*. The language style and the brevity make it particularly good for Campaign Board Members, especially if new to the area. But it is also a fine tool for the fundraiser, to help them keep Board Members on track and as a reminder of the key elements they need to practice on a daily basis.

Iain More, Founder, The More Partnership

With over 30 years of fundraising experience in the NHS and other charities I have seen both success and failure of individual projects. This handbook significantly reduce the risk of failure.

Fundraising: The Essentials for Success is an invaluable tool written in accessible style, summarising the bricks and mortar of a fundraising campaign and highlighting common pitfalls. I would recommend this book to anyone starting on a fundraising journey and all those involved with existing projects. It will enhance your understanding of the mechanics and psychology of fundraising and it is a fun to read as well. Make sure you have a copy to hand!

Anna Gregor, CBE, FRCP, FRCR

I love the style of this book. Perfect for new governors, trustees, board members and new staff, particularly in small fundraising offices. Also a good back pocket reference for professionals in the field, as it's such an easy read. I identified with so many words, phrases and mantras within these pages.

David Rider, Director of Development, Merchiston Castle School

Overall, for a new Board of a small nonprofit organisation with no experience in development, this is very helpful. It would also be useful for new School/College Advisory Board Members at universities.

Paul Elstone, Senior Associate Vice President Development, University of Oregon

Successful fundraising is often presented as some sort of dark art, beyond the reach of those who are new to it. This handbook shows that it is founded in common sense. Campaign success is achievable to us all, if we think objectively about our fundraising ambitions and are realistic about their capacity to attract financial support.

Fundraising: The Essentials for Success highlights the many pitfalls for the unwary or the inexperienced. For those with responsibility to oversee, support or actually raise the money it shows them how they can avoid such pitfalls and how they can succeed in their campaigns and build new confidence in creating change.

Sandy Richardson, Major Gift fundraiser, including V&A Dundee & National Museums Scotland

INTRODUCTION

There is a lot of money out there looking for the right home. Annual charitable giving is over $350 billion in the USA and £10 billion in the UK. But there are also a lot of charities and non-profit organisations after that money! How do you convince these potential donors to come to your particular door?

Fundraising: The Essentials for Success shows you how to put yourself in pole position: the "must dos" that will turn your campaign from an also-ran to leader of the pack.

This is the essential performance checklist for people with the responsibilty for the success of a fundraising campaign, but who are not themselves fundraising specialists: the chairs of campaign committees, trustees, the senior executives of organisations engaged in fundraising and volunteer leadership. It details the key elements of a fundraising campaign, highlights where problems can occur and explains how to overcome them.

It also provides practical support for fundraising professionals, helping them to focus the effort of the campaign board at each stage of the campaign.

25 years of hands-on fundraising experience are distilled into a concise, comprehensive guide to the absolute essentials of successful campaign creation, preparation, development and execution.

And all revealed in under an hour!

Your steps to fundraising success:

Phase 1 **Are you ready?**

The What, Why, Who and How of constructing a compelling fundraising proposition.

Phase 2 **Get set**

The essential ingredients that will ensure your campaign stands out against the competition.

Phase 3 **Go**

The co-ordination of all your resources to deliver that winning performance.

Whether it is a multi-million dollar national effort or a local programme, the challenge remains the same: how do you persuade enough people to give **you** enough money?

Here's how to do it...

PHASE 1

Get ready

Fundraising is Marketing.

Fundraising campaigns compete just like any manufactured good or service. They must stand out from the competition, promoting features and benefits that give customers satisfaction and make them want to buy.

You must know who your customer/donor is and how to engage their interest. Check that your campaign

- Has clearly identified its market ☐

- Has a proposition that excites an enthusiastic reaction ☐

- Convinces its audience it is value for money ☐

If you can't check these boxes, you will struggle.

Detailed analysis of your market, your product and its appeal is essential. Understanding your customers/donors and what they respond to is vital to the development of your proposition.

Customers normally get their satisfaction from product usage. But donating to charity doesn't generally involve direct product usage or consumption. So other ways of delivering customer satisfaction need to be examined. Understand **why** your donors give. It means you can reward them appropriately.

Fundraising campaigns fail when they focus inward on the needs of the organisation. To succeed, look outward. Identify the concerns and interests of your prospective donors, then you will know how to attract their support and their loyalty.

The essential questions – the basis for fundraising success.

The questions are deceptively simple. But you must be honest about your organisation's true capabilities when answering them. The success of your campaign depends on it.

1   **What** are you raising money for?

2   **Why** are *you* doing it?

3   **Who** is going to give?

4   **How much** a) will it cost? b) can you raise?

5   **How** will you organise your fundraising?

Answering these questions may take longer than you planned and the answers may not be exactly what you envisaged. You may have to revise your plans. Better to alter an ill-conceived plan than to deal with the financial and reputational expense of a campaign based on wishful thinking.

Investment in this first phase of preparation is crucial and will repay you handsomely.

What are you raising money for?

You are not raising money for a list of components. You are raising money to deliver benefits. So your case for support needs to explain those benefits in the context of their contribution toward your overall organisational vision.

Having determined what you want to achieve, the vital question is: does the idea appeal to prospective donors?

Be aware that how a project appeals to your organisation may differ from how it appeals to prospective donors. You need to address their specific interests.

The following example demonstrates the difference.

Organisational proposition

The new Nuclear Magnetic Resonance Scanner will excite a better resonant magnetic field emission from selected nuclei in the body. It will make us a leader in the field and enhance our research capability and reputation.

This is an organisation talking to itself and its "involved supporters", but not to most prospective donors. If their interest is not excited, they won't give.

Prospective donor proposition

"This very latest model of NMR scanner will allow us better, faster analysis of brain disease and its causes. Help us improve treatment and save lives. Someone you know may benefit."

Here is a story that many prospective donors will personally identify with and be keen to support.

You need organisational understanding to gain commitment from your team. You need donor understanding to raise funds. How your proposition is expressed depends on the audience you are talking to. It must address their specific interests.

Why are **you** the right organisation to deliver the project?

Have you the specialist expertise and track record to convince potential donors you are the best organisation to deliver the results?

It's a competitive marketplace. Donors often have a more dispassionate, and sometimes more complete, view than you do of your sector. Make sure your perception of your own capabilities and standing is realistic and not merely wishful thinking.

This is why it is really important to obtain impartial assessment of the marketplace and objective analysis of the strengths and weaknesses of your organisation.

Achieve this through a Feasibility Study (see p 33). Use it to assess your standing in the marketplace and to discover if your project has the necessary support and Unique Donor Appeal (see p 29) to succeed. If necessary, changes can be made that will improve your chances for success.

The Feasibility Study should also assess preparedness of the fundraising team to manage the campaign

It must also report on the security and accuracy of your database of potential donors and compliance with GDPR rules (General Data Protection Regulation) relating to the protection and use of personal information.

Who
are your donors?

Fundraising is not alchemy. Money is not mysteriously extracted from the ether.

Your principal sources are: Government departments (i.e. health, education, etc.); their agencies (lottery funds, arts councils, etc.); charitable foundations; wealthy individuals; public corporations; private companies and the general public.

Researching these sectors is critical to establish who your potential donors are and how much they might give. It will save you a lot of wasted time chasing pointless prospects.

Information on who gives to what is readily accessible through a variety of databases. These will help you establish which sectors contain your potential supporters and which sector is likely to give the most.

The answers to those questions will determine where you focus your effort and exactly how you present your project.

The most challenging sector in which to identify potential donors is wealthy individuals. Your organisation's donor records, if you have them, are the obvious start point. Beyond that, specialist agencies undertake wealth screening (in either instance you must understand and comply with GDPR rules regarding European fundraising). Creating a list of wealthy individuals is not difficult, but you need the answers to two vital questions: what motivates their philanthropic giving and, most difficult, how can you engage their interest?

Just because they are rich, doesn't mean they are going to give to your organisation.

How much... will the programme cost?

The answer is invariably "more than the first estimate."

(Think of how the costs of public infrastructure projects escalate, or indeed any house conversion or home improvement project you may have undertaken!)

So include a healthy contingency and double-check that all the regulatory filings and any fees and taxes of the country (VAT/sales tax, etc.) are included in the estimate.

It is much better to estimate high than low, because:

- A high figure tests the upper limits of your fundraising potential and lets you know if all or parts of your plan are achievable.

- If you underestimate you will under-pitch the amounts you request from major prospects. And, as Oliver Twist discovered, it's embarrassing and painful to go back and ask for more.

- If the cost of the programme keeps escalating it will undermine the credibility of your campaign management. "On time, on budget" are the most reassuring words for any donor.

- There is nothing more demotivating for the fundraising effort than when every €, £ or $ raised is merely playing catch-up against an ever-increasing target. It's like running up the down escalator.

How much...
can we raise?

The moment of truth – where project cost meets fundraising capability; where ambition meets reality.

The Feasibility Study (see p 33) will give you an important and impartial assessment of how compelling your proposition is, the level of interest and the size and worth of your prospective donor pool.

Believe the estimate of fundraising potential. The size and worth of the donor pool does not automatically increase just because the costs do.

If the study indicates that the financial target is beyond your immediate fundraising capabilities, you don't have to abandon the campaign. Use the "Everest strategy". Create staging posts. Divide the project into a series of lower, achievable targets and climb to your target step by step. Each successful step is a motivator for the next one.

People invest in success – your team and your donors. Using this strategy you may even over-achieve!

How... do you structure your fundraising operation?

Every campaign is unique, with its own organisational challenges.

You will need some or all of the following:

- Relentless prospect research and identification.
- Outstanding promotional design and communication strategies.
- Committed major gift fundraisers to cultivate your key prospects.
- Experienced charitable trust fundraisers.
- Excellent, secure database management.
- Top class admin to manage a public campaign, if part of your strategy.
- Enthusiastic event management teams.
- Meticulous gift management procedures for donor recognition and stewardship.

Capital campaigns, e.g. new buildings, have defined time spans and normally focus on major gifts. Donor numbers tend to be fewer, so donor communication and administrative resource are more limited. Therefore costs can represent between 10 – 15% of funds raised.

Continuous fundraising campaigns, e.g. cancer research or overseas aid, do of course attract major donors, but the main focus is on maintaining regular giving from a large donor base. Consequently the administrative investment in donor communication, event management, gift management and database management is much greater. Costs can account for up to 25% of funds raised.

Fundraising projects take time to gather traction. Contain your cost-to-income ratios by recruiting staff only as momentum develops.

Donors want their money invested in **action**, not **administrative overhead**.

Five Don'ts

It's tempting to try and speed up the campaign development process by taking a few shortcuts. But –

1   Don't begin without obtaining full organisational understanding and buy-in.

2   Don't finalise the campaign without having researched what other organisations are competing for the same prospective donors.

3   Don't make any assumptions about donor capability until you have done the research.

4   Don't set an unrealistic campaign target just to sound impressive.

5   Don't frontload your costs by recruiting the full fundraising team before the campaign is fully operational.

You should now know if you have the building blocks to launch a fundraising campaign that will withstand the rigours of public exposure.

The next section will help you shape these building blocks into a proposal with the unique appeal to make your campaign stand head and shoulders above the competition.

PHASE 2

Get set

If the fundamentals are not properly in place your campaign will be handicapped from the outset, like an athlete who has skipped some of his/her training.

The essential ingredient for success is careful preparation and planning, observing the following dictats:

Time is not on your side

The Case is the base

How to construct a Compelling Case

The Feasibility Study

Pyramid Potential

All for one

A winning team

The Campaign Board – recruitment

The Campaign Board – rules of engagement

The Campaign Board – management

Appealing communication

Connecting with donors

Public relations and public disasters

Time is not on your side

Raising money takes more time than most people imagine.

Vital time is frequently frittered away getting the campaign to the start line, because at this stage the finish line seems a long way off. However, slippage at the front end compresses the time available for the most important part of the campaign: the cultivation of prospects and bringing in the money.

Time pressure has a negative effect on fundraising. Shortened time-scales mean pressure to give is exerted on prospective donors too early in the cultivation process. They sense this. Pressure creates tensions and reduces the likelihood of the optimal outcome being achieved.

Urgency is needed right from the start. Explode out of the blocks. Get all the elements in place as soon as possible, so you have the maximum time to fully exploit all the opportunities at each stage of the quiet, public and closing phases of the campaign.

The Case
is the base

The Case is a succinct summation of your project that convinces prospective donors of its merits.

Successful fundraising is based on a concisely expressed Compelling Case with Unique Donor Appeal. It needs to excite both you and your audience. If you're not excited, why should anyone else be?

A Compelling Case is driven by the "Big Vision" of your organisation. It has a narrative that grabs the interest of prospective donors. It inspires and convinces them that they really can make the dream come true.

Unique Donor Appeal combines the attraction of an outstandingly inspirational concept with the chance to support it in a way that uniquely appeals to the individual donor.

The Big Vision might be *"Our new medical research centre will concentrate the best researchers, the latest equipment and the necessary investment to advance the search for a cure for Alzheimer's. Its outcomes will have significant benefits for a vast number of families and how they can live their lives."*

It's an expensive project. So many potential donors might feel that their donation will make little difference. But by identifying and pricing individual aspects of the project – specific research units; specialised equipment; individual treatment rooms – you can create a menu of opportunities with elements that uniquely appeal to individual donors. Now their donation has personal meaning and significance!

A big vision; a compelling case; a menu of choice – this is a cocktail with the right ingredients for success.

How to construct a compelling case

Your case is the shop window that draws in donors. It is the basis for your success. So put maximum effort into its creation.

Build it Downwards

When an architect plans a building the first concern is the overall structure not the individual rooms. Similarly, your start point is the "Big Vision" that grabs the attention of prospective donors. The individual elements that contribute to the whole proposition are developed within that.

Build it back

Fundraising is not about where you are. It's about where you want to be.

The "Big Vision" takes you to your future. It excites, it inspires, BUT it must be credible. Can you realistically bridge the gap from where you are to where you want to be? Will your prospective donors believe you? Describe your future then build the bridge back. Why is it needed? What are the major staging posts? What are the key challenges you must overcome? Will the structure and your credibility span that gap? Is it a realistic enterprise or a bridge too far?

Break it up

Your project may appear daunting in its entirety. So phase it. There are significant benefits to this approach:

- It is easier to gain support for a staged approach rather than one great leap.
- Financial targets for each element are reassuringly more attainable.
- The risk of inadequate funding is much reduced and that encourages donors.
- Individual donors feel more significant in the context of the project.
- Donors like projects where the benefit is delivered quickly.
- Success from early stages of the project creates confidence.
- Success breeds success.

The Feasibility Study

Fundraising campaigns contain both financial and reputational risk.

Use the Feasibility Study to reduce risk by assessing if:

- You have a Compelling Case with Unique Donor Appeal
- Your major prospects are favourably impressed
- Your fundraising targets are achievable
- Your organisation is properly resourced to undertake the task
- Your proposition will attract heavyweight campaign leadership

Key Issues

- Use an external agency to provide impartial assessment of your project's potential and your own preparedness. Respondents tend to be more frank than they might be if talking directly to your organisation.

- How much will donors give? Their response is the key to whether you launch the campaign. You need to believe their answers. Again prospects are more likely to reveal their true intentions when expressing opinions to a neutral source.

- Interviews with potential major prospects are essential. Over 80% of the money in major gift campaigns can come from just a few key donors. It can be difficult to achieve these interviews, but it is your one opportunity to really gauge potential support.

- Non-participation of major prospects suggests weakness in your donor relationships and creates doubt about how much money you can raise.

A general rule is that **you will convert one in three or four prospects** into donors. Cost prevents you from involving all your prospects in the Feasibility Study. So select the participants with care. Their answers and a **realistic assessment** of the larger prospect pool are **critical** to calculating your probability of success.

Pyramid Potential

The Donor Pyramid graphically presents your strategy to raise the money. It details the numbers and the value of gifts required and from whom.

The pyramid opposite demonstrates a conventional weighting between large and small gifts. Your Feasibility Study may reveal the greatest donor potential lies with a very few wealthy individuals or, conversely, amongst numerous small donors. This will determine how you structure the fundraising team.

Large donations are the key to success and are therefore your first focus for fundraising. However, major donors frequently want to see commitment from your organisation's supporter/membership group before they give. So simultaneous engagement of several audiences is often necessary. There is no standardized formula. You adapt the fundraising strategy to the demands of your particular situation.

Mid-range gifts are an important segment. But prospective donors in this bracket are generally less well cultivated. Be conservative when estimating their potential. Certainty levels drop and this segment can look like a Swiss cheese – more holes than definite prospects!

Small donors respond best when the finish line becomes visible. Now they can believe their contributions really will make the difference.

Pyramids point up the strengths and weaknesses of your prospective donor base. Research must continue throughout the campaign to identify new prospects in all donor segments. It is your insurance policy against the inevitable rejections and a source of future opportunities.

Adjust the numbers to reflect the size of your campaign and the principles still apply.

The Giving Pyramid

FUNDS
£7.85m

	Target	Cumulative

1 donor @£2 million
3 identified prospects · £2m — £2m

2 donors @£1 million
9 identified prospects · £2m — £4m

4 donors @500k
15 identified prospects · · · · · · · · · · · · · · · · · · £2m — £6m

8 donors @100k
20 identified prospects (more required) · · · · · · · · · · · · · · · £800k — £6.8m

15 donors @25k – £50k
30 identified prospects; (certainty levels reducing, more prospects needed) · · · · · · · · · £550k — £7.35m

30 donors @£10k
60 prospects (more research for prospects needed) · · · · · £300k — £7.65m

All other donors – £200K
Direct mail, telephone campaign, advertising · · £200k — £7.85k

All for one

Fundraising is a public statement of your organisation's strategic vision and ambition.

Successful fundraising enhances your reputation and creates the base for future fundraising success. The objectives of the current fundraising campaign might only benefit one or two parts of your organisation, but the whole organisation has a stake in its success.

Senior management commitment is vital. It significantly enhances the potential for success of the current campaign and therefore of future campaigns. It creates confidence within your fundraising team, your organisation and reassures and encourages potential donors.

Achieving organisational buy-in is time-consuming. It can take longer than you planned. But it is crucial that **everyone** commits to the campaign and comprehends the reputational and financial implications that may result from the campaign's success or failure.

Fundraising is hard work. The commitment of all is key to a successful outcome.

A winning team

Fundraising teams do not raise money by themselves!

Yes, it is principally their responsibility to identify and engage prospective donors. Key to this is the Director of Development, who will have experience across a range of fundraising skills, coupled with the ability to work productively with both the in-house team and the Board and motivate the fundraising team. The drive to get out and engage prospects is essential. Excellent interpersonal skills married to persuasive "proposal writing" complete the qualities of a demanding role.

But once engaged, prospects need to meet the people who will be responsible for the successful implementation of the project. They must be active advocates supported by the fundraising team.

Select the team who will best represent the project. Who will deliver the most compelling narrative? Who will provide the most convincing endorsements for the project?

The obvious candidates are those directly involved with the project. Their intimate knowledge, passion and commitment will inspire and engage prospective donors. Senior management do not have to be the principal spokespeople, but their enthusiastic support is essential to confirm top-level organisational commitment.

Campaign Board members are an integral part of the team – a strategic asset to be deployed where their intervention can favourably impress the potential donor.

Fundraisers; Executive; Board – all team members must be fully conversant with each other's roles. Co-ordinated teamwork reinforces the sense of organisational commitment that is essential for success and prospective donors always notice.

The Campaign Board

Recruitment (1)

What is the point of the Campaign Board? A question frequently asked, not just by the organisation, but also by board members frustrated by lack of clarity as to their purpose.

A well-constructed Campaign Board makes a major contribution to campaign success and requires careful pre-planning. The key appointment is the Campaign Chair. Their interaction with the organisation's senior executives and their motivating influence on the board are central to campaign success.

The recruitment of the remaining Campaign Board members requires collaboration between the Chair and the senior executives involved with the campaign. Before starting to recruit, write down the reasons for appointing members to the board and the skill sets you seek.

- What impact do you expect the board to have on the campaign?

- What geographical or professional knowledge do you need to recruit?

- What should the balance be between "the names" who add credibility and the "doers" with specific strengths?

- Most importantly: how can you ensure the Campaign Board is a productive, energising force rather than a passive, critical observer?

- How are you going to show your appreciation for their efforts and maintain their engagement and commitment?

Rules of engagement (2)

In the United States the role of the Campaign Board is summarised succinctly:

Give, get, or get out!

Beyond this rather brutal summary it's important to be specific about the rules of engagement:

- Agree in advance what you and each prospective board member expects will be their contribution to the campaign and ensure all board members understand each other's role.

- Discuss how much they will give and/or are prepared to ask contacts to give. It avoids later embarrassment. Donations from board members are essential. How can they champion the cause if they haven't given themselves?

- Establish their willingness to take part in the solicitation process and emphasise the importance of them doing so.

- Ensure they understand how they can significantly support the progress of the campaign; by identifying new prospects, thanking donors, hosting events at home or perhaps at special venues and using their peer to peer connections in ways not available to the fundraising team.

- Establish how much time they are prepared to give and over what period. (A key issue for people who are time-pressured).

The Campaign Board and the Fundraising Team need to understand the specific contribution that each will make to the campaign. Co-ordinated teamwork achieves the best results.

Management (3)

Physical board meetings are an important statement of collective commitment and energise activity. But getting board members together at the same time is often a challenge. Intermittent meetings and low attendance act like a drag anchor on activity.

There are solutions:

- The Board must be resourced for the task. But keep it lean. It makes it easier to convene and manage.

- Face to face meetings are best. The in-house team must know the board and feel its commitment. Modern technology can, where necessary, solve the need for physical attendance.

- As the campaign progresses, satellite committees can be created to support the board in specific tasks and disbanded once the objective is achieved. Time-pressured executives appreciate this cycle–on, cycle-off approach.

- This flexible approach to board management, plus the energy that comes from fresh contributions, will invigorate the interaction between the board and the in-house team.

- The mantra for board meetings is Energy, Urgency, Discipline. Meeting agendas should focus on specific issues with responsibilities delegated and timeframes agreed. Without these disciplines meetings descend into social gatherings.

A good board will advise, facilitate and open doors to prospects. Normally it is not their place to ask for money – that falls to the people directly responsible for the project. But where board members have connections with prospective donors, they should actively participate in the cultivation process.

Their committed involvement can really benefit the campaign. But the full potential is often not realised because board selection has not been properly managed. Boards that clearly understand their rules of engagement make a major contribution to the success of the campaign.

Appealing Communication

Your campaign literature is basically a calling card.

The material you produce depends on the campaign. Capital campaigns, which seek high-value donations from a select target group, can invest more in each piece of campaign literature than can a continuous appeal with its more diverse, less precise target group of smaller donors.

Brevity in brochures and leaflets

"A picture is worth a thousand words." Be visually interesting and verbally succinct. Too much campaign material, print or electronic, has too many words that mean more to you than your external audiences. What you say must be quickly understood and engage your market. Let the pictures and the headlines trigger the desire to know more which initiates that all-important personal contact with prospects.

Invest enough to do it well. The campaign literature directly reflects the values and professionalism of your organisation. Remember: fundraising is marketing.

Connecting with donors

How you choose to communicate with prospects and donors is important: broadcast media, direct mail, e-mail, social media, phone etc. **What** you communicate is vital. It must interest, involve and inspire. So you have to understand what motivates your supporters to give.

Communication strategies need long-term as well as short-term objectives. But financial imperatives often result in communication strategies geared solely to immediate fundraising objectives.

People who have previously given are your most likely source of future giving support. It is therefore in your self-interest to invest in cultivating their long-term support. But if the only investment you make is to ask them for money they will stop responding. You need input to get output. When you ask for money it is **part** of the conversation, not the **only** conversation.

One of the most powerful ways of engagement is to ask your supporters what they think of your efforts and how you might improve what you do with their money. It shows that you value them and their opinions. It makes them part of the team. It demonstrates that you do not take them or their money for granted.

Public Relations and public disaster

Your Public Relations (PR) programme is focussed on promoting the positive story, but **what happens when the story turns negative? Check your Crisis PR readiness.**

There are two immutable rules about a crisis: you can never predict its exact nature and you're never expecting it. It can de-rail your campaign.

For example: what if a CEO unexpectedly steps down, a major donor defaults, or your celebrity patron is enmeshed in scandal on the eve of your major launch? Can you cope?

Establish a Critical Risk Register. It is an essential part of the initial planning phase.

Ask: What are the possible eventualities? Who are the identified spokespeople for each situation? Who are the stand-ins when the principal spokesperson is unavailable? At what level does your CEO become involved? Have you rehearsed the scenarios and your responses?

Once a crisis breaks you have no time to rehearse or plan. The response process needs to be instant and automatic.

Successful crisis management demonstrates your organisation's professionalism. A well-managed crisis can actually enhance your status. The French phrase *"succes de scandale"* most nearly captures the opportunity that a crisis presents.

Now it's time to put your plans into practice.

PHASE 3

Go!

Your campaign is now on the start line in the best possible shape...
let's go and raise the money!

This section gives the Campaign Board insight into the processes and challenges involved in securing those gifts, so that they can maximise the effectiveness of their contribution. The Campaign Board has a key role here. Its introductions, influence, support and encouragement are essential if the campaign is to deliver its full potential.

Collaboration between the board and the fundraising team should be at its most intense. But it is at this point, if the rules of engagement were not clearly defined during the board recruitment, that this essential collaboration malfunctions. Unclear as to its role, the Campaign Board falls back on the assumption that it is the fundraising team's task to raise the money and their's simply to monitor progress. The potential of their contribution is not maximised.

Process and progress

Asking for money is outside many people's comfort zone.

There is no absolute formula that makes it easy. Much depends on the personalities of those involved. But understanding the dynamics of the process will help you navigate the path with greater certainty. Like a lot of things, the more you do it the easier it gets.

Softly, Softly

Why people give

Two ears, two eyes, one mouth

Attention please

The "5 i's"– steps to success

The Art of asking

Tax relief

Preparation or procrastination?

The Prospect Progress Chart

Fear factors

Turning it round

Love your donors

Softly, softly…

Successful fundraising is not just about knowing what the right steps are. You have to understand **when** to move, **when** to stand still, **when** to push and **when** to wait. Board members and fundraisers need qualities of interpersonal skills, empathy and intuition, persistence and patience.

The prospect pool is full of possibilities but, before you start fishing for potential donors, you need a full understanding of why they might be attracted to your particular lure. This means detailed research and careful preparation.

Even when you have attracted your prospect, the greatest chance of losing the prize is exactly when you anticipate you are about to land it. There is no particular time pressure on a prospect to give, but there is time pressure on the fundraiser to collect: a tension that can break the connection.

The need for sensitivity and patience on the part of the fundraiser applies throughout the cultivation process.

Why people give

People give to people they trust and to causes they know about, not to any random stranger.

The Campaign Board, with its reach, reputation and personal contacts, is an important constituent in establishing this recognition and trust.

People also give because:

• It actually gives them pleasure!

• They want to share their good fortune.

• They personally identify with a cause through their own experience or someone closely associated with them.

• They want to repay a debt of gratitude to an individual or organisation that has been significant in their life.

• They want to make a difference.

• They feel compassion.

• They want public recognition: to raise their status in the community.

• They wish to leave a personal memorial.

Every donor's motivation is unique. To unlock their generosity you need to understand what it is. If you don't, you might as well be speaking a foreign language or fishing with an old boot as bait.

Know your prospects. Learn everything you can about them.

Two ears, two eyes, one mouth

Use these senses in that ratio.

Learn to listen and listen to learn about your prospects – their interests, their aspirations and their attitudes to giving. Only then is it possible to understand how to help them achieve their goals.

Learn to Observe. Watch body language signals, eye contact and gestures to confirm whether what you're saying is making a connection... or not.

It's easy to get the ratios wrong, to insist on talking about your agenda rather than that of your prospective donor. It ignores the first rule of marketing: What does the customer want and how can that want be satisfied? When you know that, you can explain how what you offer meets what they want.

The Campaign Board can make an important contribution to such discussions. A potential donor will express themselves differently to someone they know well, compared to a member of the fundraising team. In such conversations vital information can be gathered.

It sounds obvious! But how many of us really listen and look to learn?

Attention please!

People have short attention spans.

You have a Compelling Case, but if you try to tell prospects the whole story you will pretty quickly bore them. They make up their minds fast. Unless they can see immediately what's in it for them, they will lose interest. **You have to grab their attention.**

So focus on the essentials in your case. What your project will achieve; why it matters to them; the key benefits; how and why it's unique. You've got 30 seconds!

This is your "Elevator Pitch". It needs plenty of practice to deliver an attention-grabbing summary in such a short timeframe. Can you do that with your current project? (see p 29 Big Vision summation as a basic guide.)

Everyone involved in the project must be pitch perfect, including the Campaign Board. They will have opportunities to interest people of influence and wealth in the campaign within their professional and social circles. There is only a moment to grab that opportunity. So the ability to present a lucid, succinct summary is essential and impresses potential donors.

It's the door-opener. Grab the attention and the opportunity for more detailed discussions will follow.

You've perfected the pitch, now it's time to introduce it to prospective donors.

The five i's – the stepping stones to success

Fundraising is a process of identification and cultivation. Throughout the process prospects fall away, until only genuine potential donors remain.

1 Identify
Research is vital throughout the campaign. New opportunities are created as the campaign develops from which research can identify new prospects.

2 Introduce
Research also reveals how to introduce the Case so it most interests your specific prospect. Not all approaches succeed, but you can use the opportunity to establish if a future approach might be more successful.

3 Interest
The introductory meeting will have revealed what sparks your prospect's interest. Now bring together the best team to ignite your prospect's enthusiasm in those areas of interest.

4 Involve
The relationship is deepened by involving the prospect in discussions of how they feel they can best contribute to the campaign goals and how they might wish their support to be recognised.

Recognition can be a complex discussion, particularly with large donations – what the donor may want versus what you can offer. Everyone must be properly briefed on what can be offered before such discussions take place.

5 Invest
This can be a lengthy process, with several meetings needed to satisfy the donor that their objectives and ambitions have been met. Most business transactions are driven by mutual self-interest. But here there is no absolute imperative for the donor to conclude by a specific date (although there certainly is for you!).

Patience and finesse are needed. Press too hard and the line will break, so the watchword is "Ready when you are!"

The Art
of Asking

The Art of Asking (1)

All the planning and preparation has been geared to this critical moment.

But most people feel awkward asking for money. It's not something they do in normal life except in a business transaction and asking for a donation doesn't feel like a business transaction.

This awkwardness can affect anyone, including senior executives and members of the Campaign Board, especially if it is their first exposure to fundraising. In fact the more senior you are the more difficult it can feel to ask. Senior people are more used to making decisions than waiting on someone else's decision. The possibility of rejection looms. And the more senior they are the more averse they are likely to be to the possibility of a public failure. This is definitely outside their comfort zone.

The fundraising team needs to be aware of the potential for embarrassment and manage the cultivation process with sensitivity to avoid this possibility: not least because saying "no" can be equally embarrassing for the prospective donor, especially if it's face to face with the top person. It damages future relations. You need to be pretty sure you know the answer before you ask the question.

Given their relationships with major prospects, senior members of the Campaign Board are likely to be involved at critical stages of the solicitation process. Their role should ideally be that of endorser rather than enforcer in closing the deal.

The Art of Asking (2)

Here are some thoughts and techniques to assist these situations.

- Asking for money is a **conversation** not a **confrontation** that arrives at a mutually acceptable conclusion.

- Have confidence. You are not cold calling. Research says that your prospect is favourably disposed. They may have given previously.

- Ask questions. Understanding their agenda is vital. Your agenda is for discussion only once you understand theirs. You can then present it in a way that stimulates their particular interest.

- Be patient. Allow plenty of time both within and between meetings for your prospect to consider things. Time pressure creates tension and reduces the chances of a satisfactory conclusion.

- Review each meeting carefully with input from all attendees. It is an an important element in the construction of the next phase of the solicitation process.

- When planning the "ask", think carefully about environment, the numbers and make-up of your team:
  - Prospects normally feel most at ease in their own surroundings. Public spaces are prone to distraction and unplanned interruption. But an impressive site visit can make a real impact and intensify a sense of partnership. Focus on what works best.
  - Don't overwhelm prospects with attendees. Two is normally better than one. More than three begins to feel like an ambush! Again circumstance dictates the decision.

- The most senior person does not have to ask for the gift, but must endorse its importance to the organisation.

- A well-managed cultivation leads to the moment when a prospect is ready to give. To avoid surprise or embarrassment ask the prospect permission to put forward a proposal at your next meeting. Your task is then to reassure them they are making the right decision.

The Art of Asking (3)

Practice makes perfect

There is one absolute rule – Practice. Practice reinforces your confidence in the proposition and confidence sells. It is so very easy to stumble at the wrong moment, particularly when talking money. It suggests you lack confidence in your proposal and introduces doubt. Be absolutely word perfect on how you ask and totally confident in what you ask for.

Rehearsal before a major ask should involve all participants including Campaign Board members. It's important that everyone knows their role. Use a devil's advocate to improve your confidence in countering any objections.

And once you have asked? Stop talking. Stay relaxed. Do not rush to fill the silence. Silence is natural. You have proposed, they are considering. It's their move. But be ready to help them if doubt or hesitation appears. The one word you are seeking to avoid is "NO". You can always meet again, because it is, after all, a conversation not a confrontation.

And don't be tempted to say: "but of course, if that's too much we would be grateful for anything". Most people, when offered a price reduction, will take it.

The more you practice the easier it gets. And the more your success rate will climb.

Tax relief

It's surprising how many donors do not fully appreciate the tax allowances that charitable donations attract.

Make sure your prospective donors understand how the tax benefits of their particular tax regime work before they decide on the gift amount. It may mean they will give more. The UK.gov and IRS.gov websites respectively contain information on charitable reliefs.

UK charities should be aware of the 501(c)(3) in the USA, which establishes charitable status and exempts donors from tax. This can be achieved by the UK organisation setting up a 501(c)(3) with its own Trustees, a majority of which should be US residents, or, possibly less expensively, by directing donors to give though an organisation such as the Charities Aid Foundation or the British Schools and Universities Foundation.

Approved American charities seeking donations from the UK can direct donors to the Charities Aid Foundation (CAF), who can advise on tax effective giving to both the USA and within Europe

Alternatively Transnational Giving Europe (TGE) also enables European residents to donate tax effectively across European borders.

Preparation or procrastination?

Detailed preparation is essential to maximise gift potential.

But preparation can become procrastination: the moment of truth delayed due to nervousness about the outcome. It can cause tension between the Fundraising Team and the Campaign Board, particularly as the finish line looms over the horizon.

The quandary is that a premature attempt to close the deal risks rejection or underachievement on gift potential. Delay, however, inhibits the development of other potential donors.

Capital campaigns can receive over 80% of their money from a few large donors. You need to be confident before casting your fly. You don't want to mishandle the one opportunity to land the prize and you know if you strike too early you can waste months of cultivation. So there is a natural tendency to delay to try to increase the certainty.

Manage this dilemma through the Prospect Progress Chart. It is the key tool for controlling the prospect management and solicitation process.

The Prospect Progress Chart

Think of the chart as progressing barges through the locks of a canal system until they arrive at the unloading point.

From Prospect to Benefactor

The Progress Chart is a complete summation of the fundraising activity. It is collated from the **individual solicitation plans** that each major prospect should have. It details each prospect, where they have reached in the cultivation process and who is responsible for them. It flags up where timescales have slipped and where assistance is needed to advance the programme.

The Progress Chart is the focal point for regular team meetings. Campaign Board members are unlikely to attend these meetings but must be kept abreast of progress, so they can contribute to the cultivation process where they have influence.

On the opposite page is a basic example of a Progress Chart. Adapt it to your own operational processes.

A few suggestions:

- Do not try to cover every prospect, at every meeting. It leads to shallow analysis.
- Prioritise prospects from each stage of the process for in-depth discussion of cultivation strategies. This is the chance to establish where board members can make specific contributions.
- Agree upon action dates and stick to them.
- Avoid holding progress meetings too frequently. It diverts time from the real focus of progressing prospects. (Monthly should suffice.)
- Resources are rarely sufficient to manage all prospects. The 12/4/1 system – make contact once per month, once per quarter, or once per year – ensures the appropriate level of attention is applied to everyone in the prospect pool.

Prospect Progress Chart

Manager	IDENTIFY			INTRODUCE		INTEREST		INVOLVE		INVEST		RESULT
	Prospect	Action	Target Date	Current Action	Target Date	Current Action	Target Date	Current Action	Target Date	Current Action	Target Date	
AB	Name: ABC Trust Gift target: £250K	In depth research	Done	Finalise Solicitation Plan and arrange prospect contacts	Successful intro complete	2nd meeting with project team. Refine interest areas	Done	Advance discussions to decide specific area of interest	Done	Finalise amount location personnel and ask	Done	Success £220K
DM	Name: TGD trust Gift target £200	Research profile Interests charitable giving	Done	Solicitation Plan and prospect contacts	Done	Assemble team for getting to know you discussions	Done	Specific areas of interest identified. Focus on exact level of interest	Done	Donor strategy. Amount, location, personnel and date to be agreed	30 Aug	
TW	Name: J Smith Gift target £100K	Research profile Interests charitable giving	Done	Solicitation Plan and prospect contacts	Done	Criteria for potential involvement established Develop proposal	Done	Meet to develop specific proposition in area of interest	25 Jun			
TW	Name: S Brown Gift target £50K	Research profile	Done	Solicitation Plan and arrange meetings	No interest Stop contact							No further action
	Name: F Khan Gift target £10K	Research profile	25 Feb	Solicitation Plan and arrange meetings	Successful intro	Refine interest areas develop plan for next meeting	10 Aug					

Fear Factors

Asking for money makes many people feel awkward, as already stated. But other factors also increase their reluctance to ask. Here are a few inhibitors:

- **An unconvincing narrative**

  You can't sell what you don't believe in, or what is plainly not convincing the prospects. No confidence in the product means no desire to get in front of the audience. Simply put: fear of failure.

- **Rejection**

  It's not nice being told no. "No" is a difficult thing to hear. It's easier to find an excuse not to ask and thus avoid hearing what you don't want to hear.

- **The last chance saloon**

  The larger the potential gift the greater the inclination to procrastinate. So much hangs on the outcome, particularly if this is the only live prospect in your prospect pool! What if they say no? Where do you go? Any reason to delay allows you to keep hope alive.

- **A sense of inferiority**

  The term "begging letter" encapsulates a misconception that fundraising is a supplicant/master relationship that relies purely on the donor's charity, because you have nothing to offer in return. It's not an effective mindset from which to convince potential donors.

Do you identify with any of these fear factors?

There are solutions...

Freedom
from fear

An unconvincing narrative

Remember: The Case is the base. If it's failing to convince your prospects, it must be reviewed. As they say, the customer is never wrong. Of course it's hard to admit that it's not working, but better to alter course than to continue paddling against the current.

Rejection

You are not being rejected. It's **not** personal.

Fundraising is a game of numbers. There are many more "no's" than "yes's". Understand that. A double-glazing salesman once told me, "I love it when someone says no. It means I am one call nearer to my next yes!"

Listen well to the "no" reasons. They often signpost an opportunity for a successful approach at another time.

The last chance saloon

Confidence comes from numbers. This is where the importance of effective research becomes clear. It delivers more prospects to your pool thereby reducing the importance of any single rejection. With back-up opportunities the paralysis induced by having only one roll of the dice disappears.

Inferiority

You are not begging. You are doing them a favour! You are offering donors a unique opportunity to make a difference, to change lives AND to feel really good about themselves. You are the bearer of fantastic news.

You have something they really want and **will** thank you for!

Love your donors

"Thank you" – the two most important words in fundraising.

You cannot thank your supporters too much. Good stewardship is vital. The better you do it the more your future fundraising will benefit.

Every fundraiser, campaign board member and senior executive connected with the fundraising campaign must know who has given and how much. Nothing is more calculated to offend than not knowing that the person you are talking to is already a donor. Only one action ranks worse: suggesting they might like to contribute!

The people most likely to continue purchasing your products are satisfied customers. A large part of their satisfaction comes from knowing how much you appreciate their support. Poor donor appreciation and stewardship will destroy all the good work you have put into attracting them.

Saying "thank you" does not stop once you have acknowledged the gift. It is most effective when you regularly demonstrate that you remember and appreciate their generosity and, through that, build a lasting relationship with them. A first donation may well be only a trial run on the part of the donor to establish if you 'deserve' a bigger gift.

It is astounding how badly some organisations treat their donors, as though the receipt of the donation is the end of the transaction. *It is only the end of the beginning.* The actual end may well be a long-term relationship of significant giving... or a substantial legacy!

Begin at the end

If your gift acknowledgement and donor stewardship are inadequate, your fundraising effort will seem like filling a sieve. Donor potential will constantly escape through the mesh.

So start your fundraising at the end of the process! Check that your organisation's rules for gift acknowledgement function with military precision.

- Have a written protocol for management of incoming gifts.

- Have specified signatories for acknowledging gifts at varying levels.

- Agree the level that the Campaign Chair or CEO becomes the signatory.

- Acknowledge all gifts within two days of receipt.

- Ensure that the Finance Department and Fundraising Team communicate; informing each other on when donations are expected or received.

- Agree with donors the amount of contact they want with you and their preferred methods of communication.

Confidence in your gift acknowledgement injects confidence into the fundraising programme.

Very last thoughts...

Legacies and Planned Giving are a very important source of funds to many charities.

But it takes at least five years to see significant results. Fundraisers tend to focus on the immediate task of achieving the targets for the current campaign. It is very possible they won't be there in five years.

The Chief Executive needs to ensure that legacy fundraising is part of the strategic plan and maintain oversight of its ongoing implementation.

We have just talked about how successful cultivation of your donors can lead to more substantial gifts and legacies. Not everything has to wait until the will is read. For major donors, well-connected with your organisation, discussions about legacies or planned giving gifts during their lifetime are a legitimate conversation. They may well be keen to discuss and plan it, so that they know that their wishes will be properly interpreted.

Knowing about the donor's long-term intentions is mutually beneficial, for their peace of mind and your forward planning. Ensure it is part of the cultivation process where appropriate.

And finally two Carnegies...

This book has one message: to succeed, focus on what interests and inspires your donors.

"You can make more friends in two months by becoming interested in other people than you can in two years by trying to get other people interested in you." Dale Carnegie

Once you have made those friends you can discuss things that interest you both!

And for those moments when you need encouragement: remember these words, from one of the world's great philanthropists.

"You are what you think. So just think big, believe big, act big, work big, give big, forgive big, laugh big, love big and live big."

Andrew Carnegie

Fundraising is hard work. To succeed have a big vision, big and passionate belief and inspire others to join in your belief. Then it is utterly rewarding.

42543344R00052

Printed in Poland
by Amazon Fulfillment
Poland Sp. z o.o., Wrocław